Jackie the Penguin Goes to America

Jackie Visits American National Parks and Learns About the Animals, Geysers, Glaciers, Caves, and Native American Tribes

An Adventures of Jackie the Penguin Book

ALEX SHALAND

GTA BOOKS • CLEVELAND

Jackie the Penguin Goes to America

The third book in the Adventures of Jackie the Penguin Series

Copyright © 2024 Alex Shaland

GTA BOOKS

All rights reserved. No part of this book may be reproduced in any form by any electronic or mechanical means including photocopying, recording, or information storage and retrieval without permission in writing from the author.

Reading age: 6 - 10 years (provided by GTA Books)

Cover by: Alex Shaland

All photographs copyright © Alex Shaland unless otherwise credited. All rights reserved. The photo on page 34 has been dedicated to the public domain by the Yellowstone Tribal Heritage Center. Photos on pages 13, 14, 30, 31, and 32 have been dedicated to the public domain by the Yellowstone National Park.

ISBN: 979-8-9876115-6-2

The author would like to express his deepest gratitude to all who contributed to this book: Jessica Burtis, Robert Berk, Carol Fox, Sandra Kramer, Sophia Muchnik, Judy Wechter, Irene Shaland, and Michelle Shaland.

Also by Alex Shaland

JACKIE THE PENGUIN GOES TO MADAGASCAR

JACKIE THE PENGUIN GOES ON SAFARI

SUBURBANITES ON SAFARI

Table of Contents

Who Is Jackie? 4
Explaining Difficult Words 5
Why We Came to America 6
The Yellow Bus and the Boring Lecture 7
Lazy Clouds and Boiling Water 8
Is This an Antelope? 10
Who Is the Fastest of Them All? 11
A Head with Two Trees 12
The Diving Deer 13
Paddle and Splash 14
This Is Not a Buffalo! 16
Say Hi to the Little Creatures 18
Is This a Wolf or a Coyote? 20
Meeting the Red Hunter 22
What Color Is the Black Bear? 24
Stay Away from the Grizzly 26
What's a Glacier? 28
Jackie Is Lost 29
A White Goat Went Up the Mountain and
Met a Sheep and a Cat 30
People Who Lived There Before 33
Where To Next? 35

Who Is Jackie?

Hi, friend! If you already read about my adventures with Irene and Alex in my earlier books, I am glad to see you again. If this is the first time we've met, may I tell you about the three of us? I am a small penguin, and I live in a place called Boulders Beach in the country of South Africa. Irene and Alex are my human friends from America. As we travel together, we love to learn about all kinds of places and wild animals here on our planet Earth.

Our first adventure together was a safari in Africa where we met many awesome animals. Then, Irene and Alex took me to the island of Madagascar. I loved the huge baobab trees, cute lemurs, colorful chameleons, and all kinds of other creatures. I also understood how important it is to care about the nature of our planet. In this book, I will tell you about our adventures in three American national parks: Yellowstone, Grand Teton, and Glacier National Park. "And how did you, a small penguin, get to all these places so far away from your home?" you might ask. Easy! I flew in airplanes!

Did I tell you that flying in airplanes is awesome? As a bird who could not fly, I always envied seagulls, cormorants, and other birds who could glide through the air high in the sky. But me, I just stood there on the ground and imagined what an amazing view they had. Then one day, my human friends, Irene and Alex, took me on an airplane flight over Africa, and all of a sudden, I was flying way higher than any bird ever could! It was so cool! I was on my way to see the world.

Explaining Difficult Words

While listening to Irene and Alex, as well as park guides, I've learned so many new words during my adventures, and I am dying to tell you what they mean right now. Knowing these difficult words will help you understand what I am talking about in this book.

The word **wilderness** means a place where no people live, like a forest. The word **backcountry** pretty much means the same – an area where no or very few people live. An **ecosystem** is an environment where plants and animals depend on each other and the changes that happen in nature throughout the year.

Habitat means a special kind of nature where certain plants and animals live. For example, the parks we visited have several different habitats: **forest**, **alpine** (mountains), **sagebrush** (dry, rocky land), **grassland** (fields covered with grass), and **wetland** (areas near rivers and lakes). Every habitat has special plants and animals that live there.

To my surprise, I've learned that some animals sleep through the winter and don't eat or drink until spring! People say that these animals **hibernate**. Speaking of animals, **wildlife** is a name for wild animals that don't live together with people. **Mammals** are animals that feed their babies with milk. **Carnivores** eat meat. **Herbivores** eat plants. **Predators** are animals that hunt other animals (called **prey**) to eat them. And the word **species** is another name for a large group (or kind) of similar living organisms. A male and a female of the same species join as a family and have **offspring** (another word for babies).

National parks are parts of the land where plant life and animals are protected. **Plant life** means trees, bushes, grass, flowers, and so on. A **field guide** is a book with pictures that help you identify wildlife and other things of nature. **Indigenous people** are the original people who live or used to live in a certain place. The letters **cm** stand for centimeters, **m** means meters, **km** means kilometers, **g** means grams, and **kg** is short for kilograms.

If later on you forget what some of these words mean – no problem! Just come back to this page and find them here.

Are you ready to go on an adventure? First, I will tell you why my friends and I visited the American National Parks.

Why We Came to America

"Why would you and Alex want to go to all these American parks if you already live in America?" I asked Irene. Irene explained that the United States of America is a huge country, and she and Alex traveled mostly to big cities located in the east. But now, they wanted to see the land and wildlife in Yellowstone, Grand Teton, and Glacier National Parks in western states called Wyoming, Montana, and Idaho.

"We will see majestic mountains, beautiful lakes, fantastic hot springs, mudpots, fumaroles, geysers, and glaciers like nowhere else in America! That's not to mention the wild animals roaming free across the fields, forests, and mountain slopes," Irene got so excited that she almost yelled while waving her hands and smiling.

"Wow," I said, "I don't know what most of the things you said are, but I can't wait to see them and learn all about these wonderful places from you and Alex. Alex is okay, but I really like Irene, especially when she patiently explains to me things I don't know or understand. Take a look at one of the pictures Alex took in Grand Teton National Park. You will understand why Irene was so excited.

The Yellow Bus and the Boring Lecture

All three parks are so huge that we needed a car to drive around to see some of the coolest spots and look for wild animals. So, when our airplane landed, Alex rented a car at the airport and drove us to Yellowstone National Park and later to other parks. But in Yellowstone, it was way cooler to ride in a funky yellow bus that took visitors all around the park. The bus driver was also a guide who knew everything about nature and animals. Alex finally had a chance to take photos any time he wanted, which was not an easy thing to do when he was driving our car.

Our first adventure started in one of these yellow buses. When we were in our seats, the guide (also called a park ranger) told us about Yellowstone history. Listening to him go on and on was boring, so, I will just tell you a few things I remember.

Many years ago, in 1872 to be exact, the American government took approximately 3,500 square miles (9,000 square km) of land and called it a public park, which later became the Yellowstone National Park. Most of the new park was in the state of Wyoming and a little in the states called Montana and Idaho.

It was done to protect the awesome nature and wildlife from hunters, **prospectors**, **loggers**, and **settlers**. Prospectors look for **minerals** (stuff in nature that did not come from animals or plants) in the ground; loggers cut down trees to make all kinds of things from the wood; and settlers also cut down trees to make fields where they grow crops and pastures where their cattle can graze. All these human activities would have destroyed nature. The American government wanted to preserve this land, so that it wouldn't be destroyed and visitors like us could come and enjoy the natural beauty of the park year after year.

Finally, the yellow bus began to rumble and we went on our first adventure!

Lazy Clouds and Boiling Water

When our yellow bus climbed to the top of a hill, I looked down into a valley below us and, to my surprise, saw a large cloud resting on top of a big puddle of water.

"Wow!" I exclaimed. "I have never seen a cloud come down from the sky and rest on water. Is it too lazy to fly? And the colors below it are so crazy: blue in the middle and bright orange around it. What am I looking at?"

"Actually," the guide said, "what looks like a cloud is steam rising from the water." He then explained that we were looking at the Grand Prismatic Spring – the largest hot spring in the world.

Hot spring.

"And how come the water is so hot that it makes steam?" I asked. What I learned then was amazing! There is a huge volcano deep underneath Yellowstone National Park. Water from the surface seeps down below through cracks in the ground. Way deep down, there is super hot **molten** (liquid) rock called **magma**. Magma heats the water coming from above and turns some of it into steam. Then, the steam pushes hot water back up to the surface through the cracks. In some places, the hot water comes out (like in **hot springs**), but in other places only steam comes out. And that is how nature creates **hot springs**, **mudpots**, **fumaroles**, and **geysers**. I found out that Yellowstone has lots of all of those, more than anywhere else.

As for the crazy colors – the minerals in the water make it look bright blue. The orange color comes from some silly bacterium (called **thermophiles**) that love hot water! That bacteria can do whatever it wants, but I sure would not want to swim in this steaming water.

In **fumaroles**, only hot steam comes out through holes in the ground. **Mudpots** have some water but also weird stuff that our guide called **sulfuric acid** and tiny microorganisms. And the acid smells bad! The acid and microorganisms are such bullies that they turn rocks into clay and mud! On the next page, you can see a fumarole at the top and a mudpot below it.

Fumarole.

Mudpot.

Jewel geyser.

Old Faithful geyser.

Honestly, watching this mud and steam was pretty boring. But later I was finally able to see geysers, first a small one called the Jewel Geyser and then, the most famous one called Old Faithful.

When hot water tries to come to the surface in a **geyser**, it can't because the passage is blocked. But, the steam keeps pushing, and finally, the blockage opens and the water squirts up in the air (or erupts). The Old Faithful geyser erupts approximately every hour and water jumps as high as 150 feet (45 m).

This was all very interesting, but I also wanted to see the wild animals of America. That is why I came here in the first place! Finally, the yellow bus brought us back to our lodge, and Irene, Alex, and I started discussing what to do next.

Is This an Antelope?

"Okay, guys. We've spent enough time watching jumping water and doing nothing. Let's go look for interesting things – the animals!" I said. "You are right, let's go to our car," said Alex, "Who is driving, you Jackie?" "Very funny, just get in the driver's seat, Alex," I said and jumped in my seat next to Irene.

"This animal looks like a mule deer," said Alex after looking at a brown animal standing under a tree and then at a page of an open book he took from Irene. I replied, "First of all, it does not look like a mule, and second, who did you call 'dear', me or Irene?" "This animal is a deer with a double 'e' and it is called the mule deer because its ears resemble the ears of a mule," said Alex, confusing me even more.

"Next question," I said, "What is this book you keep looking at?" Alex replied that the book was called a **field guide**. It had pictures and descriptions of the animals and other things we would see in the parks.

After Alex gave the field guide back to Irene, she read to us that the mule deer was also called the "jumping deer" because it likes to jump really high when it runs. Mule deer weigh between 200 and 300 pounds (90 to 140 kg). The males have antlers on their heads, which they shed (drop) in winter. The new antlers start to grow in March. The female mule deer don't have antlers.

"Hmm, this is strange." I thought. "Why would a deer drop its antlers? Don't they need them in winter? I will ask Irene about it next time I have a chance."

Who Is the Fastest of Them All?

"Jackie, do you want to see the fastest runner in America?" asked Alex when he stopped our car on the road surrounded by an open field. Then, he pointed at a small group of animals that looked kind of similar to some antelopes I saw in Africa. "Are they antelopes?" I asked. Alex said, "People call them American antelopes, but actually, they are not part of the antelope family." Alex confuses me a lot.

Then, Irene explained that these animals are called pronghorns. They weigh 80 to 150 pounds (36 to 68 kg) and are between 2.5 and 3.5 feet (0.8 to 1.1 m) tall. Some females have small horns, like the one on the right. The horns of the adult male you see below are big and fancy, with prongs (points) facing forward. Those prongs on the horns give the animal its name.

Horns have bony inside covered with keratin (stuff that hair and fingernails are made from). The same pair of horns stays on the head of the animal for life.

Pronghorns live in groups called herds and love to hang out in wide-open grassy fields. They are not good jumpers, but if a wolf or a coyote approaches, pronghorns sprint at over 40 miles per hour (64 km per hour). Even their babies (called fawns) are fast. Only two days after it is born, a fawn pronghorn can run faster than Alex. A four-day-old fawn could easily win a race against a horse!

I had no interest in chasing after these pronghorns – I am a champion swimmer, not a sprinter. So I was eager to find out who we would meet next.

A Head with Two Trees

"Why is this big antelope carrying two small trees on its head?" I asked Alex after he stopped our car. "First of all, this animal, called an elk, is not an antelope, it's a deer. And second, those are not trees – they are antlers," Alex replied. "Antlers are made of bone and have branches. Animals that have antlers shed them every year," added Irene who always knows how to explain things to a small penguin.

She said that though elk are big, not all of them are the same size. The smaller ones weigh about 500 pounds (230 kg), but the largest elk could grow as huge as almost 1,500 pounds (680 kg)! They prefer to hang out close to a forest for safety.

"Why do elk drop their antlers like the mule deer do?" I asked. Irene's field guide said that the male elk, called bulls, shed (drop) their antlers in winter or early spring. And soon, the new antlers begin to grow, bigger than before. "Aha, now I understand," I thought.

"And why do male elk need such huge antlers," I asked, "to fight bad animals who want to hurt them?" "Sometimes," said Irene, "but mostly, they fight each other." "Why are they behaving so badly?" I exclaimed. Irene said that the strongest bull will make a family with the most beautiful females, called cows. And later, they will have baby elk, called calves.

"Did Alex have to fight other boys when he wanted to marry you, Irene?" I asked. "Yes, he did," she giggled.

The Diving Deer

"Why is this strange animal standing knee-deep in the river?" I asked. Irene's field guide said that we were looking at a moose, the largest species of the deer family. A moose can weigh between 700 and 1,400 pounds (318 to 635 kg) and be 6 to 9 feet (1.8 to 2.7 m) long. That makes it a little bigger than the elk and much bigger than the mule deer, both of which you read about before. By the way, the words "elk" and "moose" can mean either one animal ("one elk") or many ("lots of elk").

Moose don't like being in a group and are usually alone as they move about in rivers and lakes. They love willows that grow close to the water. And often, moose are wandering knee-deep in the water. Why? Because they also eat vegetation that grows on the bottom of rivers and lakes. "A moose can dive almost 20 feet (6 m) and stay underwater for half a minute," said Irene.

"Ha," I laughed, "I can dive 100 feet (30 m) deep and stay underwater for 2 minutes!" "Yes," said Alex, "but you are a penguin, and this is a moose."

"You are right," I agreed, "but who else can we find around rivers and lakes?"

Paddle and Splash

Beaver.

Otter.

According to Irene's field guide, one such animal is called a beaver. Adult beavers are close to 4 feet (1.2 m) long and weigh about 70 pounds (32 kg). And you would not believe what they eat – leaves, twigs, and tree bark! Beavers use mud and sticks to build their home in marshes (areas where land is covered by water), creeks, and ponds. Then, they build a dam to create a pond around their home to protect it from predators. "Smart beavers!" I thought.

Another animal that lives in large rivers and lakes is called a river otter. It is about the same size as the beaver – about 4 feet (1.2 m) long. Otters eat fish and dive for up to two minutes to catch them. When it is time for a mama otter to give birth to her baby, she will look for an abandoned beaver home or make her own home under a tree stump. The newborn baby otter does not know how to swim, so the mama otter has to teach it.

The first bird on the next page, called the American white pelican, also catches fish for dinner, but it does not dive into the water. Instead, while swimming, the pelican scoops up fish in its large throat pouch, squirts out the water, and then swallows the fish. This bird is big. If you include its huge beak, then this bird can be 50 to 70 inches (130 to 180 cm) long. Pelicans weigh between 11 and 20 pounds (5 to 9 kg). And, unlike a penguin like me, pelicans can fly. When they spread their gigantic wings, pelicans can glide through the air like there is nothing to it.

American white pelican.

Canada goose.

Female mallard duck.

Male common merganser.

Another big bird is the Canada goose you see below, but it is smaller than the pelican. Not all varieties of this goose are the same size. A Canada goose can be between 25 and 40 inches (64 to 100 cm) long and weigh from 6 to 9 pounds (2.7 to 4 kg).

Irene's field guide said that Canada geese eat grass or water plants that grow on the bottom of lakes, rivers, and ponds. So, you will usually find them in fields or on water.

At the bottom of this page, you can see two water birds: the female mallard duck on the left and the male common merganser on the right. Mallard ducks weigh between 1.5 and 3.5 pounds (0.7 to 1.6 kg). This species is called the dabbling duck because its feet are attached to the body at its center, which makes keeping balance and walking a piece of cake for this bird. Common mergansers are a little larger, and their feet are further back to make it easier for these birds to dive. Well, it's time for us to get back on dry land and look for more interesting animals.

This Is Not a Buffalo!

When we stopped to look at an enormous animal eating grass close to the road, I asked Alex: "When we saw these animals in the distance, sometimes you called them buffalo and other times bison, why?" "The correct name is bison, but people often call them buffalo," Alex replied and added that there is even a famous song, *Home on the Range*, that starts with the words: "Oh give me a home, where the buffalo roam."

From Irene's field guide, we learned that these huge animals can be as tall as 6 ft (1.8 m) and weigh more than 2,000 pounds (900 kg). Bison are the biggest mammals in North America! Being so big, they need to eat a lot of grass, which they do most of the day. They live in groups called herds, and older females are often in charge of the herd.

"Can I pet this nice bison?" I asked. "No way!" exclaimed Alex, "Don't be fooled by their size and lazy walk, and never come too close to a bison." I learned that a bison can run as fast as 35 miles per hour (56 km per hour). And if it catches up with you, you will be in big trouble – just look at that huge head with a pair of mighty horns.

We did get very close to these giants. All traffic stopped because a huge bison stood right in the middle of the road and would not let any car pass him.

Finally, after whining for several days, Alex had a chance to snap a few close-up pictures of a bison. Alex was happy, but I felt scared: this animal was bigger than our car!

"Alex, you told me to never get close to a bison!" I protested, "And look where you brought us now!" "What can I do?" Alex replied, "The bison is in front of our car, and other cars are behind us."

And then, another bison walked in from the other side of the road. Great! Two huge bison and I am in the car between them! Now I was really scared.

When the bison finally went to eat grass, and we were free to go, I said: "Okay you guys, so far I have only seen animals that are much bigger than me. What about the creatures that are smaller than a little penguin? Can you find some of them for me?"

Say Hi to the Little Creatures

I asked Alex to put pictures of several small creatures in this book so that you can see how they look. Irene found their names in her field guide.

First, we found a white-tailed jackrabbit hiding in the bushes. It was very shy and hopped away as soon as we came close. It is a little bigger than me (an 18-inch tall penguin) – over 20 inches (50 cm) long. Unlike me, this jackrabbit is a very fast runner. If a wolf or a fox comes close, the jackrabbit will sprint and run zigzag as fast as 35 miles per hour (55 km per hour). To be less noticeable, these animals change the color of their coat: brown in summer and white in winter. During the day, they hide under the bushes and come out at dusk to eat grass and green plants.

White-tailed jackrabbit.

The smallest creature we found was called the least chipmunk. Not counting the very long tail, a chipmunk's body is only about 5 inches (12 cm) long – much smaller than me. It has gray stripes on its back and white stripes on its face. Look at the two pictures below. When this chipmunk runs, its tail points up, like a flagpole. In winter, this tiny animal hibernates (sleeps).

The least chipmunk, front and side.

When I saw the next little creature, I thought it was a big chipmunk. But Irene said that it was a golden-mantled squirrel. Just look at the picture on the right and the two pictures at the bottom of the previous page. Notice the difference?

The chipmunk has white stripes on its face. The golden-mantled squirrel on the right has white circles around its eyes. And both of these animals have the same way of carrying food home: they stuff seeds, nuts, and other food behind their cheeks. And then, when they come home, they spit the food out. Their home is called a burrow (a fancy name for a hole in the ground). The squirrel is a little larger than the chipmunk: about 7 inches (18 cm) not counting the tail. It also hibernates in the winter.

Golden-mantled squirrel.

The Uinta ground squirrel has no stripes at all. But, boy, can this animal sleep! Not only does it sleep in winter, but it goes back to its place and falls asleep (hibernates) in the middle of summer when this squirrel feels that it is too hot. Compared with the creatures above, it is a little bigger, growing up to 9 inches (23 cm) long, not counting the tail.

Uinta ground squirrel.

The body of the red squirrel at the bottom of this page is about the same size as Uinta's – up to 9 inches (23 cm) long. But its tail is much longer. Unlike other creatures on this page, red squirrels love climbing trees. And when they jump from branch to branch, the squirrels use their tails to change direction, like the rudder of a ship.

Red squirrel.

Chipmunks and squirrels are all **rodents**, just like mice and rats, but look pretty friendly. Other animals we met were much bigger and often very scary, at least from the point of view of a little penguin.

Is This a Wolf or a Coyote?

"Is that a wolf?" I asked Alex, pointing at a gray animal in the middle of a field covered with tall grass. "Irene said that wolves are very dangerous and, compared to me, they run very fast," I said, "So, I think we should not go close to it. Alex, you and your camera can do whatever you want, but Irene and I are staying in the car."

Looking at her field guide, Irene said that in Grand Teton National Park, it is possible to see both wolves and coyotes, but she could not tell which of the two carnivores (animals that eat meat) we were looking at.

The field guide said that spotting a coyote was no big deal because they like open fields and might even come close to the road. But wolves like to stay out of sight, so we only had a small chance to see a wolf.

Irene also said that the gray wolves that live in this park, weigh anywhere from 80 to 130 pounds (36 to 59 kg) and are 25 to 35 inches (63 to 89 cm) tall – the size of a big dog. The colors of a wolf's coat are mostly white, black, or gray. And sometimes, you can see a little bit of brown fur.

But coyotes are much smaller than wolves, about one-half of their size, and their coat is more colorful. If you see a wolf-like animal with fur that is tan, light brownish-yellow, and gray with a rusty color on the back of the ears, then you probably spotted a coyote, not a wolf.

The heads of these two animals are also slightly different. A coyote has more pointed ears and a narrower nose compared with a gray wolf. Both coyotes and wolves often live in groups called packs. But, it would not be unusual to see a lone animal going about its chores.

"Did you know, Jackie," asked Irene, "that domestic dogs came from wolves?" She said that thousands of years ago, people tamed some wolves, and that is how the dog species started. "Do you mean that a tiny chihuahua and a huge Saint Bernard dog come from the same animal – the wolf?" I exclaimed in disbelief.

"Yep, that's evolution for you Jackie," said Alex and added that "evolution" is how animals and humans changed over thousands of years.

"Visitors often can't tell if they are looking at a wolf or a coyote when they see the animal from a distance," said Alex, "Jackie, can you tell if this is a wolf or a coyote?"

"I can't see clearly," I replied: "Irene, could you please hold your binoculars in front of my eyes? My flippers are good for swimming and poking Alex, but they are useless for holding things." "Okay, I see a narrow nose and pointy ears with some brown on them. I guess, it's a coyote," I said. "I agree," said Irene looking at a picture in her field guide, "I hope we can also find a wolf and compare the two species."

Later that day, a guy in a pickup truck next to our car pointed at an animal standing on a dead tree and said that it was a gray wolf. Look at both pictures on this page. Can you see the difference between the coyote above and the wolf below? To be honest with you, I can't. Just don't tell Alex – he will make fun of me again, and I don't like it!

"Let's go and look for other predators!" said Alex.

Meeting the Red Hunter

"Who are those **predators** Alex was talking about?" I asked Irene. Irene always takes the time to explain things to me. So, she said that predators are animals that hunt other animals (called **prey**) and eat them. "Like lions that we saw in Africa?" I asked. "Yes," said Irene, "but the predators that we can find here are wolves, coyotes, foxes, brown and black bears, and cougars."

I already saw a coyote and a wolf but had no idea what the other predators looked like. One thing is for sure: I hoped that we would be inside our car or the yellow bus when we met other scary predators, but that is not what happened later that day.

When we returned to the camp, it was already getting dark. Irene went inside our cabin, but Alex and I stayed outside just a little bit longer. Then, I noticed some movement on the deck of the cabin next to ours.

We moved closer and found ourselves face to face with a beautiful, furry creature staring at us. "Red fox," whispered Alex and snapped a picture.

I recalled that foxes are predators, but I was not afraid, not at all! "Why?" you ask. Because Alex was standing next to me, and he would protect me if I were in danger. The fox turned around and went into the woods, and we ran to our cabin, opened the door, and taunted Irene: "We saw a fox, we saw a fox! And you did not!"

You should have seen Irene's face! But no worries, she also had a chance to see a fox the very next day. This time, a fox was marching in broad daylight and totally ignored us. So, we had all the time in the world to observe it. Meanwhile, Irene opened her field guide and started reading us some facts about the red fox.

    These animals are actually small, only 9 to 12 pounds (4.0 to 5.5 kg), but because of their long legs and thick fur, they appear bigger. Both foxes we saw had yellow, gray, and white fur on their heads and bodies and black fur on their legs. But Irene said that some red foxes do have brownish-red fur, which gave this animal its name.

    Foxes live alone, not in groups, and they like open fields with a few trees nearby. But, as we found out, sometimes they don't mind living close to people. Honestly, I can't say that I felt at ease next to a predator, even as small as a fox. Remember, I am only 18 inches tall and can't fly. So, I secretly hoped that the next animal we find would be a bit friendlier. No such luck!

What Color Is the Black Bear?

"Me, walk through the woods? No way, unless Alex carries me in his backpack," I said and stomped my feet. And sure enough, Alex did. We were preparing for our first expedition on foot, and walking was not my favorite way of getting around.

After about an hour of walking and looking at boring trees, bushes, and grass, our guide turned to us and said: "Make noise, like singing or talking loudly. We don't want to surprise the black bear that was spotted nearby earlier today." "Oh, no! Please, don't let Irene sing!" I protested. "Alex is kind of okay, but if Irene starts singing, even bears will run away! She can't carry a tune if her life depended on it!" "Well," said the guide, "then talking loudly will probably do." "You don't even have to ask for it," chuckled Alex. "Okey-doke," agreed Irene, "I will just cry, 'Hey bear!' when I feel a little scared – which is now."

After just a short walk, my poor head began to ring because of Irene's constant warning calls. But, since safety comes first, I said nothing. Finally, we spotted a brown animal in the distance walking slowly across a grassy field covered with beautiful blue and yellow flowers. "Please meet your first black bear," said the guide. "But this bear is brown, not black!" I muttered. "Animals that belong to this family are called black bears. But actually, they come in many colors: black, brown, and even blonde," explained our guide.

I learned that black bears can weigh anywhere from 100 to 300 pounds (45 to 135 kg), and the males are usually much bigger than the females. Unless a mama bear has her babies (called cubs), black bears are solitary, which means that each adult bear lives by itself.

The next day, we did see a black bear that was actually black. This time, we were inside a big yellow bus, and the guide spotted a bear standing close to the road we were traveling on. When the bus stopped, I turned to Alex and said: "Alex, this is your chance to take a decent bear picture. Now you can't complain that the bear is too far, the bus is driving too fast, or that it is too dark to take a good picture."

"Are black bears very dangerous?" I asked our guide. "Yes, but they are not as aggressive as the other kind of bear we did not see today," he replied. "What American animal might be scarier than this bear," I thought. The next day, I found the answer to my question.

Stay Away from the Grizzly

We were in our car when I spotted a big brown furry animal standing in the tall grass. "Is this a black bear with brown fur, or a different kind of bear our guide was talking about?" I asked Alex. "It sure is brown and looks different from the black bear we saw yesterday. The one that was actually brown, but the guide told me that it was a black bear." "Yep," Alex replied, "It's a grizzly for you."

"Alex, I asked you if this was a brown bear. But what's a grizzly?" I protested. Alex kept confusing me, as usual. Then, Irene explained that grizzly bears are part of the brown bear family found all around the world. In America, they are called grizzly bears.

And do you know which animal was the scariest one of all we met during this adventure? The grizzly bear! They are not friendly at all and are very aggressive. If you see a grizzly mama with a cub or two, stay as far away from them as you can. But the male grizzlies are not much nicer, and they are big.

These bears weigh between 250 and 600 pounds (110 to 300 kg). And when one of them stands up (something they do a lot) it can be as tall as 8 feet (2.4 m)!

Even the black bears usually stay away from the bigger and stronger grizzlies. When you take a look at the grizzly's huge front paws with claws that can be as long as 4 inches (10 cm), you will understand why. Watch out, Alex, you are no match for this grizzly bear!

I said: "Alex, why don't you give a couple of your favorite Reese's peanut butter cups to this grizzly? Maybe then it will be nice to us and come closer, so that you can take a good picture." "Jackie," said Irene in a very serious voice, "You must never, ever feed wild animals!" Then, she explained that if a bear gets used to human food, it might start demanding food from park visitors. And this might end badly for the visitors and the bear. "Alex," I demanded, "no snacks or candy bars in your pockets, please!"

Thank you very much, I have seen enough scary animals for one day and was ready for some relaxing vacation time. So, I said, "Hey guys, how about driving around and enjoying some of the amazing views around us?"

What's a Glacier?

I forgot to tell you that we met all the bears in Glacier National Park. "Why is this place called Glacier National Park?" I asked Irene, "I don't see any glass here." Irene, who, unlike Alex, always takes the time to explain things to me, said that the word "**glacier**" describes a huge sheet of ice that grows on the side of a mountain. Way up there, it is so cold all year long that snow in the valleys does not melt, even in summer. As more and more snow keeps piling up, the weight of this snow pushes down on the snow below it turning snow into ice.

One day, the sheet of ice becomes so heavy that the glacier starts sliding down the mountain slope. Not fast – the glacier moves from about 5 to 30 feet (1.5 to 9 m) in one year.

"Can you show me a glacier?" I asked. Alex pointed his finger at a mountain in the distance and told me that the white cover on the mountainside was a glacier.

"I wish I could see a glacier up close, but there is absolutely no way I am climbing that mountain," I said.

Then, Alex showed me a picture of him standing next to a glacier. Irene had taken this photo during their trip to a country called Iceland. Can you see how thick that glacier was? But I could not believe my ears when Irene told me that the thickest glacier in Glacier National Park was 500 feet (150 m) thick!

Do you want to hear how I got lost during one of our adventures? Read about it on the next page.

Jackie Is Lost

On the way to Glacier National Park, we made a stop to explore a cave called the Lewis and Clark Caverns. I had never been inside a cave before, so I felt a little nervous. But when the guide led us through a door right inside a mountain and turned on the light switch, I forgot all my fears.

"Wow!" I cried, "Who made this magical cave underground?" Our guide explained that about 300 million years ago, this area was at the bottom of the ocean. When small creatures living inside shells died, they fell to the bottom. Over time, their shells, along with corals, formed layers of soft stone called limestone.

Millions of years later, the water level of the ocean went down, and the limestone became buried underneath the surface of the earth. Then, rainwater containing some nasty stuff called acid started seeping down through all kinds of cracks in the ground. Little by little, this acidic water began dissolving (turning from solid into liquid) the limestone it touched. And that's how water created this limestone cave.

The guide was going on and on, and, without knowing it, I fell asleep at the bottom of the steps I was sitting on. When I opened my eyes, I could not see anything! I guess the only light inside the cave came from the electric lights, which the guide turned off when everyone, except for me, left the cave. Honestly, I freaked out not being able to see in the dark.

Then, the lights came on again, and I saw Alex rushing down the steps towards me. When he brought me outside, I said: "I was not scared at all. I know that you and Irene would never leave me in trouble! But no more caves, please! Right now, I want to relax and enjoy the sun."

A White Goat Went Up the Mountain and Met a Sheep and a Cat

After the scare inside the cave, we finally arrived at our lodge located inside Glacier National Park. Later that day, I was enjoying a lovely sundown on the terrace overlooking a beautiful lake at the foot of the rocky mountain. All of a sudden, Alex yelled, "I see a mountain goat!" and pointed at the top of the mountain. As hard as I looked, I saw nothing, which was very frustrating! "You need very strong binoculars to see this crazy goat," said Alex.

So, I had to ask Irene to hold her binoculars for me and then, I saw it. Irene's field guide said that this animal is one of the alpine species, meaning that it lives in the mountains. "And why would these silly goats climb all the way up the mountain?" I asked: "I don't see much grass there, just rocks, which they can't eat. Why not go to the lake where there is plenty of juicy green grass?"

Irene explained that mountain goats are afraid of the wolves and coyotes that can catch them in the fields. So, they find the steepest slopes of the mountain and look for whatever little grass, plants, and bushes they can find. And no wolf in its right mind would climb a rocky wall no matter how hungry it is.

"And if even wolves can't climb this mountain, how come the mountain goats can?" I kept asking. Irene's field guide said that the goat's legs are very strong and have hooves with soft pads on the bottom. These hooves can spread and grab the rocks when the goat is climbing up or down the mountain.

Irene's field guide also said that the biggest male goat can be as tall as 39 inches (1 m) and weigh as much as 250 pounds (113 kg). And can you believe this: only 10 minutes after it is born, a baby goat called a "kid" can stand up, run, and jump? The kid in the picture on the left is older of course, but still...

The mountain climber goat is not the only animal with hooves that does not mind steep rocky mountain slopes and is not afraid of heights. The bighorn sheep like to hang out above ten thousand feet and can easily jump from rock to rock on an almost vertical wall. Their hooves with rough bottoms can stand on a thin ledge, which is only 2 inches (5 cm) wide!

Mountain goats and bighorn sheep are approximately the same size. Males of both species are larger than the females.

Irene's field guide also said that the bighorn sheep's name comes from huge spiral horns you will see on the head of an older male sheep called a ram (like the one in the picture). The ewes (females) have smaller, straight horns. Irene said that you can tell if the male sheep is young or old by looking at its horns: smaller, less spiral horns – you are looking at a young guy; larger, more spiral horns – it's an older dude.

If you think that after climbing high up the mountains these animals are completely safe from predators, you will be sad to learn that it is not so. Irene said that one particular animal, the mountain lion, is not a vegetarian at all, and it can climb! Mountain lions were spotted as high as 19,000 feet (5.8 km), according to Irene's field guide.

This large cat species is also called cougar, panther, and puma. The biggest mountain lions can weigh almost 200 pounds (90 kg), and if you count the tail – be 8 feet (2.4 m) long. It runs pretty fast, but prefers hiding in the trees and bushes and then pouncing on an unsuspecting prey. Watch out you goats and sheep!

All this climbing and jumping, Irene kept reading about, made me feel dizzy. I am a penguin, so the only jumping I like is jumping in the water. So at that point, I was ready to jump into my bed and think about the next day. Enough mountains for one day!

People Who Lived There Before

While traveling through the parks, we met very special people called **park rangers**. They were wearing a uniform, so you could easily spot them. Irene explained that there are all kinds of different rangers: some of them tell visitors about the park; other rangers lead groups of visitors on walks and rides and tell them about nature; and some rangers are responsible for the safety of visitors and animals, similar to police officers. If a visitor becomes ill or injured, rangers will rescue them. I was sure glad to learn that park rangers would be there for me if I needed help!

Everywhere we went, in our car or on foot, there were many people around us. Most of them had cameras, just like Alex, or binoculars, or just cell phones. And they all watched and photographed the animals and the beautiful nature all around us.

"All these people are visitors who came to enjoy nature and watch the animals, right?" I asked, "But where are the people who live here?"

And then, I learned about the **Indigenous people** of America, people who began living on this land a long time ago, before people from other places came and settled there. Irene opened one of her books and read to me and Alex about the history of Yellowstone and the people who lived in this area before the American government declared it a national park. In 1872, the government established a national park on a huge part of the land they called the Wyoming Territory. Politicians (people who hold government offices) wanted to preserve nature and create a park where people from all over America and other countries could visit and enjoy the woods, geysers, lakes, waterfalls, canyons, and, of course, wildlife. Nobody – including the Indigenous people who had lived there – would be allowed to hunt, gather berries and fruits, cut trees, or change nature in any other way inside this park.

But, for more than ten thousand years, people of the **Native American Tribes** have been living in that area. They depended on the land for hunting, gathering, and traveling. The tribes called the Sioux Indians lived there. Members of the Sheepeaters, Crows, Bannocks, Shoshone, and Blackfeet tribes traveled through the Wyoming Territory. They met with each other and eventually European settlers to trade goods. So, to create a wilderness park, people of these tribes were told by the government to move from the area designated for the park to other places.

"So, today, park visitors don't know anything about the people who used to call these lands their home but live in other places now?" I asked Irene. "That used to be true, but hopefully not anymore," she replied and told me that in 2022, a brand new Yellowstone Tribal Heritage Center was built not far from the Old Faithful Lodge, the hotel where we stayed while exploring Yellowstone.

The center has a photography exhibit and presents all kinds of programs for visitors. Members of different tribes tell stories, dance in their traditional costumes, and do other fun things. "I love learning new things, so this center would be an interesting place to visit," I thought.

When Alex and I were writing this book, we asked the nice people who work at the Yellowstone Tribal Heritage Center to share a photo showing one of these events so that we can include it in this book and you can see it for yourself. Here is a photo of a boy from the Nez Perce Tribe performing one of their traditional dances. When you come to Yellowstone, make sure you visit the center – it is a cool place and you can learn so much about the history of the land and the people who lived there for thousands of years.

Where To Next?

And then, the day of our departure back home finally came. We took our last picture in the park and drove to the airport. "So, where to next?" I asked my friends while we were waiting for my flight back home in South Africa.

"Aren't you tired of trotting around the globe with us?" asked Alex. "No way!" I exclaimed, "I want to see more cool places and animals." "Well, there is one big cat – the tiger – that I absolutely have to see in the wild," said Irene. "We chased it in Nepal but had no luck. So, our next expedition is to India, where, I am sure, we will meet the Royal Bengal tiger. Do you want to come with us? We can pick you up on the way to India."

"Are you kidding me?" I said. "Of course! I want to go with you everywhere, except maybe boring places like big cities, museums, and monuments that you guys keep talking about."

I told Irene and Alex that I would be waiting for them at the usual place – my home in South Africa. This time, I had no doubt that they would not forget about me – I am their friend, and who forgets about their friends? And besides, I am so smart, handsome, and lovable that going on an adventure without me would not be much fun at all.

Note from Jackie and Alex to our young readers:

We hope that, while reading this book, you enjoyed meeting the amazing animals of America, learned about the wonders of the natural world that draw visitors to American parks, and glimpsed into the past of several Native American Tribes.

Happy reading and learning!

www.ingramcontent.com/pod-product-compliance
Lightning Source LLC
LaVergne TN
LVHW070535070526
838199LV00075B/6786